And Play

By
Pamela Conn Beall and
Susan Hagen Nipp

Illustrated by
Nancy Spence Klein

PSS!
PRICE STERN SLOAN

"Me first! Me first! . . .
There must be a better way."

Choosing Rhymes

Choosing rhymes determine who is It. One member of the group chants the rhyme while pointing to the children one by one, himself included. By one method, the child pointed to on the last word is It. By another, he is out and the rhyme is repeated until one child is left to be It. Mother Goose rhymes can also be used as choosing rhymes.

EENY, MEENY, MINY, MO

Eeny, meeny, miny, mo,
Catch a tiger by the toe.
If he hollers, make him pay
Fifty dollars every day.
My mother told me to
Choose the very best one.

Variation:
Eeny, meeny, miny, mo,
Catch a rabbit by the toe.
If he hollers, let him go,
Eeny, meeny, miny, mo.

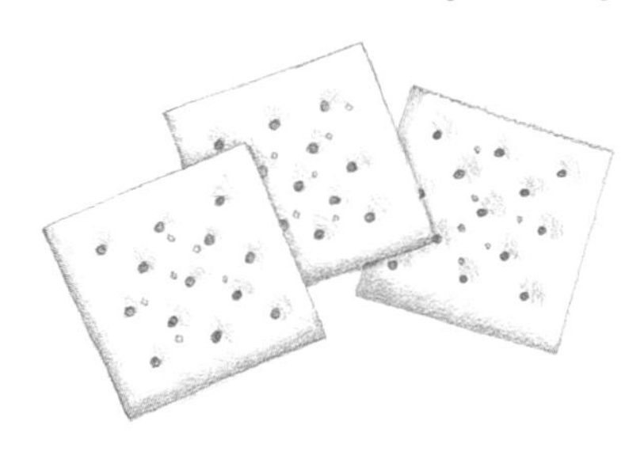

ICKY, BICKY

Icky, bicky soda cracker,
Icky, bicky boo,
Icky, bicky soda cracker,
Out goes you!

HOT POTATO

One potato, two potato,
Three potato, four,
Five potato, six potato,
Seven potato, MORE.

Formation:
Children stand in a circle or line with their fists held out in front of them. One child is It.

Action:
- It pounds each fist in turn, including her own, in rhythm.
- The child whose fist is pounded on the word "more" places that fist behind his back.
- This continues until one fist remains. That child is the winner.

I CAUGHT A FISH

One, two, three, four, five,
I caught a fish alive.
Six, seven, eight, nine, ten,
I let him go again.
Why did you let him go?
Because he bit my finger so.

APPLES, PEACHES

Apples, peaches, pears, and plums,
Tell me when your birthday comes.

"March!" M-A-R-C-H

Variation:
"March!" January, February, March

Action:
- The child pointed to on "comes" names the month of his birthday.
- Pointing continues as the month is spelled out. The child pointed to on the last letter is It.

FIREMAN, FIREMAN

Fireman, fireman, number eight
Hit his head against the gate.
The gate flew in, the gate flew out,
That's how he put the fire out.
O-U-T spells OUT
And out you go.

ONE, TWO

One, two,
Sky blue,
All out (in)
But you!

ENTRY, KENTRY

Entry, kentry, cutry, corn,
Apple seed and apple thorn.
Wire, brier, limber lock,
Three geese in a flock.
One flew east, one flew west,
One flew over the cuckoo's nest.
O-U-T spells out goes she (he).

A, B, C, D

A, B, C, D, E, F, G,
H, I, J, K, L, M, N, O, P,
Q, R, S, T,
U are out!

MARY AT THE KITCHEN DOOR

One, two, three, four,
Mary at the kitchen door.
Five, six, seven, eight,
Mary at the garden gate.
O-U-T spells out!

BUBBLE GUM

Bubble gum, bubble gum in a dish,
How many pieces do you wish?

"Five!"   1, 2, 3, 4, 5 and out you go.

Action:

- The child pointed to on "wish" answers with a number.
- The rhyme continues by counting to that number.

Suggestion:
Children hold their fists out in front for the leader to pound.

ENGINE NUMBER 9

Engine, engine, Number 9,
Going down Chicago Line.
If the train goes off the track,
Do you want your money back?

"No!"   N-O spells no, and out you go!
or
"Yes!" Y-E-S spells yes and out you go!

Action:

- The child pointed to on "back" answers "yes" or "no."
- The rhyme continues by spelling "yes" or "no" as above.

"It's party time! . . . Now what?"

Circle and Singing Games

THE FARMER IN THE DELL

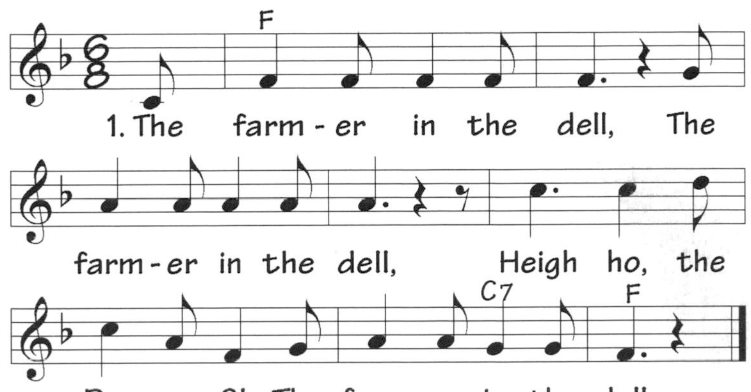

2. *The farmer takes the wife . . .*
3. *The wife takes the child . . .*
4. *The child takes the nurse . . .*
5. *The nurse takes the dog . . .*
6. *The dog takes the cat . . .*
7. *The cat takes the rat . . .*
8. *The rat takes the cheese . . .*
9. *The cheese stands alone . . .*

Formation:
Children stand in a circle, hands joined. One child, the *farmer*, stands in the center.

Action:
- Children circle around the *farmer*.
- On verse 2, the *farmer* chooses a *wife* to join him in the center of the circle.
- The game continues until the last verse, when all but the *cheese* return to the circle.
- The *cheese* becomes the *farmer* for the new game.

Suggestion:
Those inside the circle may circle around within the larger circle.

THE SEED CYCLE

(Tune: The Farmer in the Dell)

1. *The farmer sows his seeds . . .*
   (farmer scatters seeds; seeds spread out inside circle)
   Heigh ho, the Derry O! The farmer sows his seeds.
   (seeds curl up on the ground)
2. *The wind begins to blow . . .*
   (wind players run about waving arms)
3. *The rain begins to fall . . .*
   (rain players run about, fingers hanging down to indicate raindrops)
4. *The sun begins to shine . . .*
   (sun players walk slowly, arms in circle above head)
5. *The seeds begin to grow . . .*
   (seed players slowly rise, becoming grain)
6. *The farmer cuts his grain . . .*
   (action as with scythe; grain falls to ground)
7. *The farmer binds his sheaves . . .*
   (farmer touches three at a time, who stand back to back)
8. *And now the harvest's in . . .*
   (all skip around sheaves, hands joined)

Formation:
Before the song is begun, divide group into *seeds*, *wind*, *rain*, *suns*, and one *farmer*. The children form a large circle. Inside the circle are the *seeds* and the *farmer*.

Action:
Each group pantomimes the words of its verse inside the circle. The children return to their places in the circle, except *seeds*, who always remain in the center.

Suggestion:
Simplify by having all children pantomime all parts.

THE NOBLE DUKE OF YORK

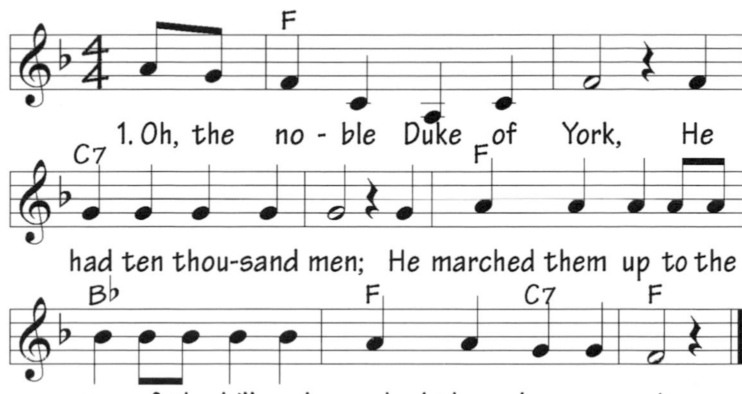

2. *And when you're up, you're up,*
   And when you're down, you're down,
   And when you're only halfway up,
   You're neither up nor down.

3. *Oh, a-hunting we will go,*
   A-hunting we will go;
   We'll catch a little fox and put
   him in a box,
   And then we'll let him go.

Formation:
Children sit in chairs or squat.

Action:
Verse 1
- "10,000 men"—raise arms full length, fingers outstretched
- "up"—stand
- "down"—sit

Verse 2
- Repeat actions for "up" and "down"
- On "halfway"—assume crouching position

A-HUNTING WE WILL GO

GAME 1

Use verses 1 and 3 of *The Noble Duke of York*.

Formation:
Children stand in a circle, hands joined. One child as the *fox* stands outside the circle.

Action:
Verse 1
- Children circle to the left as the *fox* skips to the right.

Verse 3
- The two children nearest the *fox* lift their arms and force him into the circle by bringing their arch down behind him.
- The children slowly close the circle to trap the *fox*.
- On "let him go," the children raise their arms and let the *fox* escape.
- He chooses another *fox* and the game begins again.

GAME 2

Use verse 3 of *The Noble Duke of York*.

Formation:
Children form a line of pairs with a head couple.

Action:
- The head couple leads the other couples as they march across the room, sepa rating at the end, one line going right and the other left.
- The lines march back to the other end where the partners meet.
- The head couple forms an arch through which the other couples march. This creates a new head couple and the game continues until all partners have been the head couple.

PUNCHINELLO

2. *We can do it, too . . .*
3. *You choose one of us . . .*

Formation:
Children stand in a circle, one child in the center as *Punchinello*.

Action:
Verse 1
- *Punchinello* makes a motion as the others sing.

Verse 2
- Children in the circle copy *Punchinello*'s motion.

Verse 3
- *Punchinello* chooses another child to be in the center and takes that child's place in the circle.

THE HOKEY POKEY

1. You put your right hand in, you put your right hand out,

You put your right hand in and you shake it all a-bout,

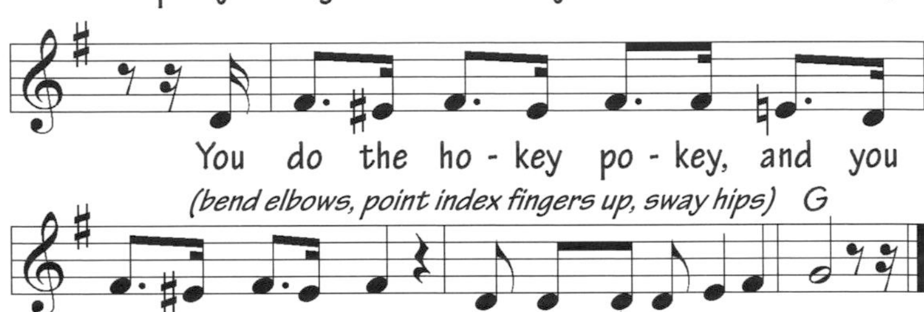

turn your-self a-round, That's what_ it's all a - bout!

(clap in rhythm)

2. *You put your left hand in . . .*
3. *. . . right foot in . . .*
4. *. . . left foot in . . .*
5. *. . . right shoulder in . . .*
6. *. . . left shoulder in . . .*
7. *. . . right hip in . . .*
8. *. . . left hip in . . .*
9. *. . . head in . . .*
10. *. . . whole self in . . .*

Formation:
Children stand in a circle.

Action:
Follow the actions of the words.

THE MUFFIN MAN

2. *Oh, yes, I know the muffin man . . .*
3. *Now four of us know the muffin man . . .*
4. *Now we all know the muffin man . . .*

GAME 1

Formation:
Children stand in a circle, hands joined, one child in the center.

Action:
Verse 1
- Children circle around the child in the center.
- At the end of the verse the child in the center chooses a partner.

Verse 2
- The children circle around the two in the center. At the end of the verse, the two in the center choose two more.

Verse 3
- Children circle around the four in the center.
- At the end of the verse, the four choose four more. Repeat verse 3, changing the number each time until all are in the center.

Verse 4
- All children join hands and circle around.

Game 2

Formation:
Children stand in a circle, hands joined. One child is blindfolded in the center.

Action:
Verse 1
- The children sing as they circle around the blindfolded child.

Verse 2
- The children stop circling.
- The blindfolded child points to a child who then sings the song alone.
- The blindfolded child has three tries to guess who sang alone.
- If correct, the soloist becomes the blindfolded child. If incorrect, the game begins again with the same blindfolded child.

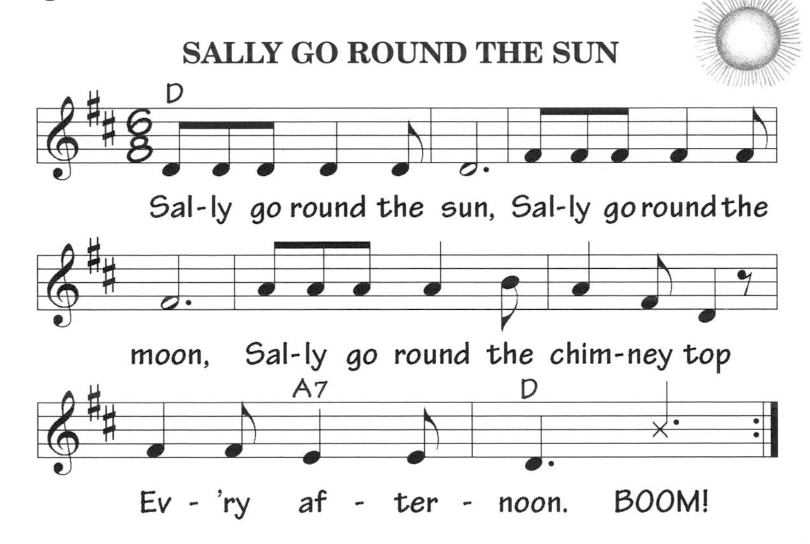

Formation:
Children stand in a circle, hands joined.

Action:
- Children circle around.
- On "BOOM," the children jump up and reverse direction to immediately start circling and singing the song again.

DROP THE HANDKERCHIEF

(Tune: Yankee Doodle)

Formation:
Children stand in a circle. One child is It and stands outside the circle, holding a handkerchief.

Action:
- As children sing the first three lines, It walks around the circle.
- It sings or chants the last line until she decides to drop the handkerchief behind a child and say, "but he will bite you."
- It then races around the circle.
- The new child picks up the handkerchief and runs in the opposite direction. Both children race to the empty space in the circle.
- The last child to the space is It.

ROUND THE VILLAGE

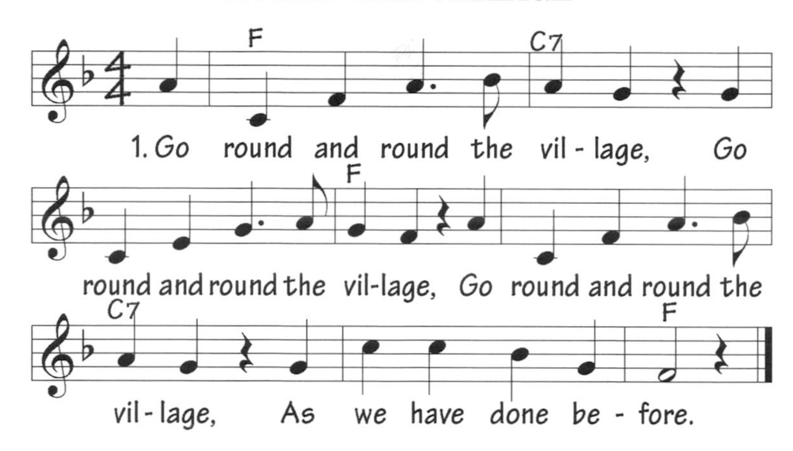

2. *Go in and out the window . . .*
3. *Now come and face your partner . . .*
4. *Now follow me to London . . .*

Formation:
Children stand in a circle, hands joined. It stands outside the circle.

Action:
Verse 1
- It skips or runs around the circle.

Verse 2
- Children in the circle raise their arms to form arches while It weaves in and out.

Verse 3
- It chooses a partner and stands facing him.

Verse 4
- It leads his partner in and out of the circle.

Verse 1
- It returns to the circle and his partner becomes It.

Suggestion:
For a shorter game, use only verses 2 and 3. The partner immediately becomes It.

LONDON BRIDGE

Chorus (sung after each verse)
Take the key and lock her (him) up, lock her up, lock her up,
Take the key and lock her up, my fair lady.

2. *Build it up with iron bars . . .*

3. *Iron bars will bend and break . . .*

4. *Build it up with silver and gold . . .*

GAME 1

Formation:
Two children join both hands and form an arch. They secretly decide who is *silver* and who is *gold*. The other children form a single line to pass under the *bridge*.

Action:
Verse 1
- The children in line pass under the *bridge*.
- On "my fair lady," the *bridge* falls and captures a *prisoner*.

Chorus
- The *bridge* gently sways the *prisoner* back and forth.
- At the end of the chorus, the *prisoner* is secretly asked, "Do you want to pay with *silver* or *gold*?"
- The *prisoner* then stands behind the child representing his choice.
- The game continues with verses and chorus until all children have been captured.
- A tug-of-war between *gold* and *silver* ends the game.

Suggestion:
Children may choose other forms of payment, such as cake or ice cream, marbles or jacks, etc.

GAME 2

Formation:
Same as Game 1.

Action:
- Same as Game 1 through the choice of *silver* or *gold*.
- At this point, the *prisoner* takes the place in the *bridge* of the child representing his choice.
- The child who was part of the *bridge* joins the line and the game continues.

BLUEBIRD

Formation:
Children stand in a circle, hands joined and raised to form arches. One child, the *bluebird*, stands outside the circle.

Action:

- The *bluebird* weaves in and out of the circle.
- On "Oh, Johnny, I am tired," the *bluebird* taps another child on the shoulder.
- The child tapped becomes the new bluebird as the first child takes her place in the circle.

Suggestion:
Let the new child choose what kind of bird she wants to be.

THE MERRY-GO-ROUND

(Tune: Mulberry Bush)

Formation:
Children stand in a circle, hands joined.

Action:
- Children circle around while singing.
- On the word "collapsed," all children fall down.

DID YOU EVER SEE A LASSIE?

GAME 1

Formation:
Children stand in a circle, hands joined. One child is in the center.

Action:
- Children circle around the lassie (laddie).
- On the words "this way and that," the lassie performs an action of her choice.
- The other children stop circling and imitate the action until the end of the song.
- The lassie chooses a new child and the game continues.

GAME 2

In place of the word "lassie," the child chooses what she wants to be, such as a *farmer* (pretend to feed chickens), *airplane* (fly), *tree* (sway gently), *elephant* (swing trunk).

JIMMY CRACK CORN

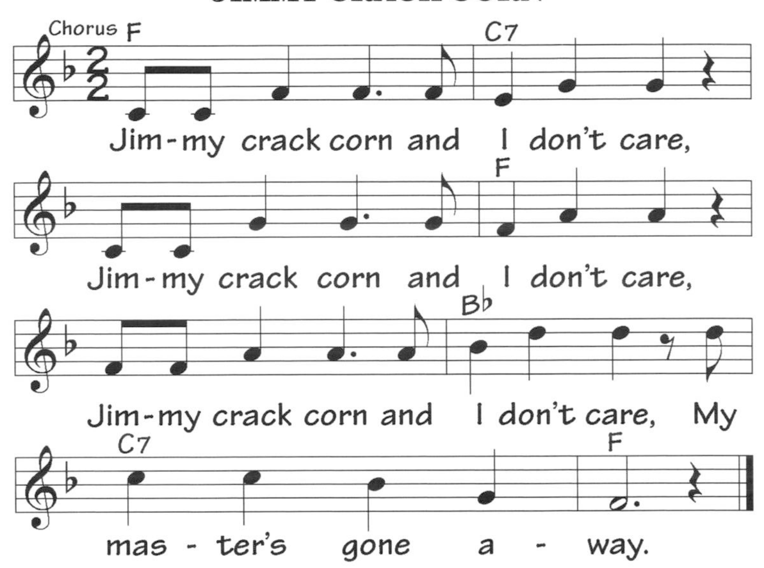

1. *Right hand up and I don't care . . .*
   (Chorus after each verse)
2. *Left hand up . . .*
3. *Both hands up . . .*

Formation:
Children stand in a circle, hands joined.

Action:
Chorus
- Children circle to the left (do after each verse).

Verse 1
- With right hands raised, children move to the center of the circle, touch hands, and move back quickly on "My master's gone away."

Verse 2
- Same as verse 1, using left hand.

Verse 3
- Same as verse 1, using both hands.

A-TISKET, A-TASKET

Formation:
Children form a circle. One child is chosen to be It and stands outside the circle, holding a handkerchief.

Action:
- As children sing, It skips around the outside of the circle.
- Sometime during the words "I dropped it," It drops the handkerchief behind any child he chooses.
- It then races around the circle.
- The new child picks up the handkerchief and runs in the opposite direction. Both children race to the empty space in the circle.
- The last child to the space is It.

SKIP TO MY LOU

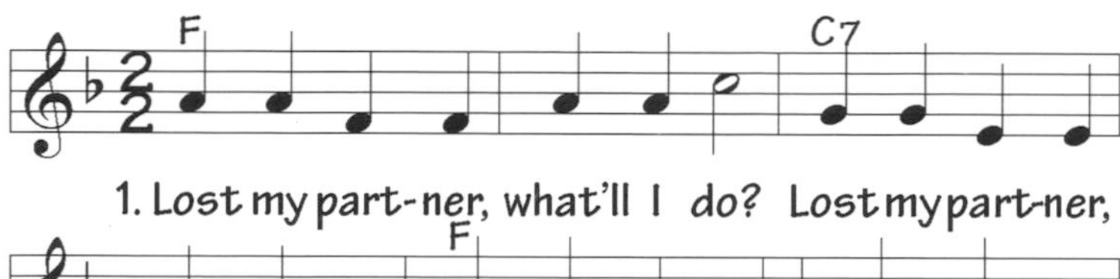

Chorus (sung after each verse)
Lou, Lou, skip to my Lou,
Lou, Lou, skip to my Lou,
Lou, Lou, skip to my Lou,
Skip to my Lou, my darling.

2. *I'll get another, a better one, too . . .*
3. *Can't get a redbird, a bluebird'll do . . .*
4. *Cat's in the buttermilk, skip to my Lou . . .*
5. *Fly's in the sugar bowl, shoo, fly, shoo . . .*

Formation:
Children stand in a circle. One child is It inside the circle.

Action:
Verses 1-5
- Children sing and clap as It skips inside the circle.
- On "Skip to my Lou, my darling," It chooses a partner.

Chorus
- It and her partner skip inside the circle, holding hands.
- On "Skip to my Lou, my darling," It returns to the circle and her partner becomes the new It.

OATS, PEAS, BEANS

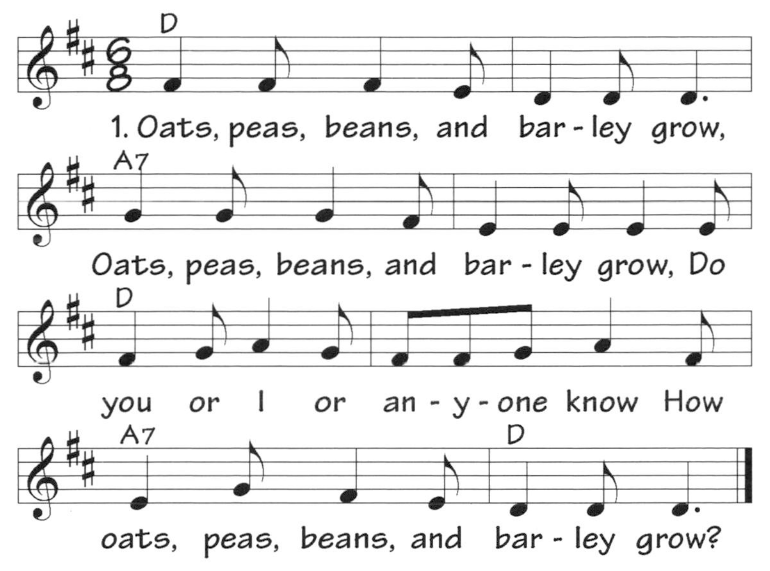

2. *First the farmer sows his seed,*
   (scatter seed)
   Then he stands and takes his ease,
   (fold arms)
   Stamps his foot and claps his hand,
   (stamp) (clap)
   And turns around to view the land.
   (turn and shade eyes)

3. *Waiting for a partner,*
   Waiting for a partner,
   Open the ring and take one in,
   And then we'll gaily dance and sing.

4. *Tra la la la la la la . . .*

Formation:
Children stand in a circle, hands joined. One child, the *farmer*, stands in the center.

Action:
Verse 1
• Children circle to the left while the *farmer* walks to the right inside the circle.
Verse 2
• The *farmer* and the children act out the words.
Verse 3
• Children in the circle stand and clap their hands as the *farmer* chooses a partner.
Verse 4
• The *farmer* and his partner skip to the right inside the circle. Children join hands and circle to the left.
• To play again, the partner becomes the new *farmer*.